LIVES
AND
TIMES

Walt Disney

Wendy Lynch

Heinemann Library
Chicago, Illinois

Published by Heinemann Interactive Library,
an imprint of Reed Educational & Professional Publishing,
100 North LaSalle, Suite 1010
Chicago, IL 60602
Customer Service: 888-454-2279
Visit our website at www.heinemannlibrary.com

Designed by Ken Vail Graphic Design, Cambridge, England
Illustrations by Alice Englander
Printed in Hong Kong / China
03 02 01 00
10 9 8 7 6 5 4 3 2

Library of Congress Cataloging-in-Publication Data

Lynch, Wendy, 1945-
    Walt Disney / Wendy Lynch.
       p. cm. — (Lives and times)
    Includes bibliographical references and index.
    Summary: A simple biography of the man who began his career as an
animator and gained world wide fame as the creator of Mickey Mouse,
Disneyland, and Disney World.
    ISBN 1-57572-671-8 (lib. bdg.)
    1. Disney, Walt, 1901-1966—Juvenile literature. 2. Animators—
United States—Biography—Juvenile literature. [1. Disney, Walt,
1901-1966. 2. Motion pictures—Biography.] I. Title. II. Series:
Lives and times (Des Plaines, Ill.)
NC1766.U52D546 1998
791.43'092—dc21
[B]
                               97-51775
                                 CIP
                                 AC

Acknowledgments
The Publishers would like to thank the following for permission to reproduce photographs:
Aquarius Library/Walt Disney Co: pp. 10, 18, 19; James Davis Travel Photography: p. 17; John Frost
Newspaper Library: p. 20; Chris Honeywell: p. 21; Wendy Lynch: p. 22; Robert Opie Collection: p. 11;
Popperfoto: p. 23; Spectrum Colour Library: p. 16.

Cover photograph reproduced with permission of Walt Disney Co/The Ronald Grant Archive.

Our thanks to Betty Root for her comments in the preparation of this book.

Every effort has been made to contact copyright holders of any material reproduced in this book.
Any omissions will be rectified in subsequent printings if notice is given to the publisher.

Some words are shown in bold, **like this**. You can find out what they mean
by looking in the glossary.

Contents

Part One

Walt Disney was born in Chicago, Illinois, in 1901. At school, he liked art best. He liked drawing cartoons.

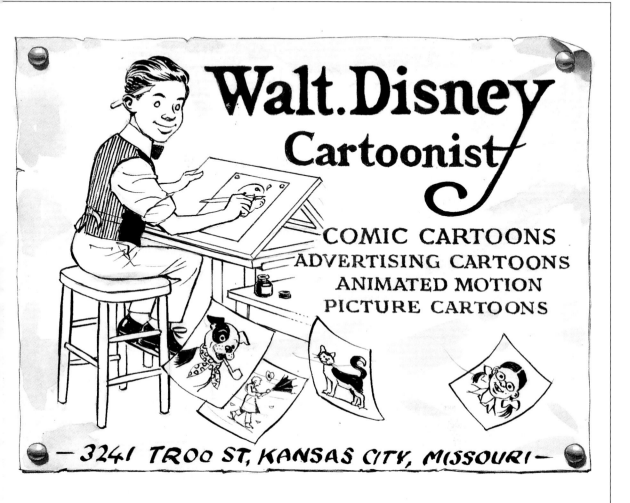

When he was eighteen, Walt worked for a company that made films. In the evenings, he made his own cartoons at home. He called these cartoons Laugh-O-Grams.

Walt drew many pictures and took photographs of them with a special camera. When he made the photos into film and played them quickly, the pictures looked as if they were moving. This is called animation.

In 1923, Walt moved to **Hollywood** to
make cartoons with his brother Roy. They
bought an old building and called it the
Walt Disney **Studio**. This is how the Walt
Disney Company began.

In 1928, Walt and a friend created a cartoon **character** named Mickey Mouse. Mickey Mouse became very famous. So did other characters, such as Minnie Mouse, Donald Duck, Pluto, and Goofy.

The first two Mickey Mouse cartoons were **silent**. Walt worked very hard to learn how to add sound to his films. Soon he learned how to use his own voice for Mickey Mouse.

Films were made in black and white because people did not know how to make films in color. In 1932, film makers began using a special camera to make movies with color. Walt also started making his films in color.

Mickey Mouse cartoons were very popular with children and grown-ups. Walt began to **merchandise** Mickey Mouse toys, comics, and watches.

One year later, in 1933, Walt began to use music in his cartoons. He recorded the music first and then made the cartoons move in time to the music. *The Three Little Pigs* was the first cartoon made like this.

At first, his cartoons were very short. Then Walt started to make longer films, like *Snow White and the Seven Dwarfs*, *Bambi*, *101 Dalmatians*, and *Mary Poppins*. He won 32 **Oscars** for his films.

Walt had many new ideas for **entertainment**. His next idea was to build a **theme park** for whole families to enjoy. Disneyland opened in California in 1955.

Walt wanted to open another theme park in Florida, called Disney World. In 1966, he became ill and died just before it was finished. Many people were sad because they had enjoyed his work so much.

Part Two

There are many ways to find out about Walt Disney. You can see his cartoons at movie theaters, on TV, or on videos. His company still makes films, such as *The Lion King* and *James and the Giant Peach.*

Besides Disneyland and Disney World, the Walt Disney Company also has a **theme park** in Europe, near Paris, France. It is called Euro Disneyland. Another Disney theme park is in Asia, near Tokyo, Japan. It is called Tokyo Disneyland.

People took many photos and made many films about Walt. This photo shows him in the **studio** where *The Mickey Mouse Club* television show was made.

Walt used posters to show which of his films were playing at theaters. Here is a poster for *Pinocchio.*

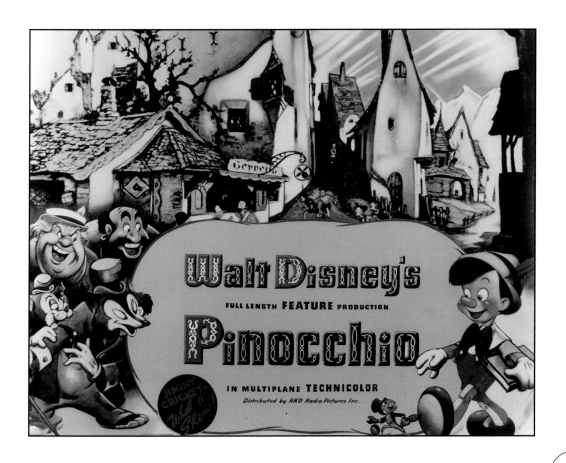

There were many stories in newspapers about Walt's life and work. Libraries keep copies of old newspapers for people to read.

Writers have written many **biographies** about Walt's life. This book tells us how he made his cartoons.

The Disney Company has opened Disney Stores all over the world. These shops sell books, toys, and videos about Walt and his cartoon **characters**.

There is a street in London, England, called Disney Street. This shows how important many people think Walt Disney is. Here is a photo of Walt and his wife, Lily, on Disney Street.

Glossary

biography book about a person

character person or animal in a film, story, or play

entertainment ways of getting people to have fun

Hollywood city in California where many movies are made

merchandise to sell things that have the name or picture of a famous character or company on them

Oscar golden statue given as an award each year to the best movie, actor, or other person who makes films

silent having no sound

studio place where films, recordings, or radio and TV shows are made

theme park amusement park based on famous characters, films, or events

Index

More Books to Read

Dell. *The Story of Walt Disney.* New York: Dell, 1989.

Hammontree. *Childhood of Famous Americans: Walt Disney: Young Filmmaker.* New York: Simon & Schuster Children's, 1997.

Selden, Bernice. *The Story of Walt Disney: Maker of Magical Worlds.* Milwaukee: Gareth Stevens, 1996.